ARCTIC ANIMALS

REINDEER

by Anastasia Suen

AMICUS | AMICUS INK

fur

hoof

Look for these words and pictures as you read.

antlers

legs

Reindeer live in the Arctic.
It is cold and icy there.

fur

See the fur?
It is hollow.
It keeps the reindeer warm.

antlers

See the antlers?
New ones grow each year.
Boy reindeer have them.
So do girls!

See the hoof?

It is furry on the bottom.

Reindeer do not slip on ice.

hoof

See the legs?
Reindeer can walk far.
The herds look for food.

legs

It is spring!
A baby calf is born.

Spot is published by Amicus and Amicus Ink
P.O. Box 1329, Mankato, MN 56002
www.amicuspublishing.us

Copyright © 2020 Amicus.
International copyright reserved in all countries.
No part of this book may be reproduced in any form without written permission from the publisher.

Library of Congress Cataloging-in-Publication Data
Names: Suen, Anastasia, author.
Title: Reindeer / by Anastasia Suen.
Description: Mankato, Minnesota : Amicus/Amicus Ink, [2020] | Series: Spot arctic animals | Audience: K to Grade 3.
Identifiers: LCCN 2018048665 (print) | LCCN 2018049062 (ebook) | ISBN 9781681518381 (pdf) | ISBN 9781681517988 (library binding) | ISBN 9781681525266 (paperback)
Subjects: LCSH: Reindeer—Juvenile literature. | Animals—Arctic regions—Juvenile literature.
Classification: LCC QL737.U55 (ebook) | LCC QL737.U55 S84 2020 (print) | DDC 599.65/8—dc23
LC record available at https://lccn.loc.gov/2018048665

Printed in China

HC 10 9 8 7 6 5 4 3 2 1
PB 10 9 8 7 6 5 4 3 2 1

Alissa Thielges, editor
Deb Miner, series designer
Ciara Beitlich, book designer
Holly Young and Shane Freed, photo researchers

Photos by Shutterstock/Sylvie Bouchard cover, 16; Alamy/Manuel Lacoste 1; Alamy/Juergen Ritterbach 3; NatGeoCreative/Suzi Eszterhas 4–5; Alamy/imageBROKER 6–7; ScienceSource/Mark Boulton 8–9; Dreamstime/Dmitry Chulov 10–11; AgeFotostock/Marc Rasmus 12–13; iStock/sarkophoto 14–15